ROBBEN FC

CW00539572

PLAYIN' THE BLUES

Editor: Aaron Stang
Additional Text by Aaron Stang
Transcriptions by Dave Hill
Cover Design: Joann Carrera
Photography: Pages 26 & 49 by Daniel Shea
           All Others Courtesy of Jeff Rivera

CONTENTS

Part I: *Scales For Blues Soloing*

Example 1: G Minor pentatonic 4

Example 2: Solo Demonstration over a G7 Vamp 6

Example 3: G Minor Pentatonic with the Added ♭5th (the Blues Scale) 8

Example 3A: Five Fingerings for the G Blues Scale 8

Example 4: Solo Demonstration of the Blues Scale 10

Example 5: G Minor Pentatonic with the Added 6th 12

Example 5A: Five fingerings for the G Minor Pentatonic 12

Example 6: Solo Demonstration of the G Minor Pentatonic with the Added 6th 14

Example 7: Solo Demonstration Using All Three Scales 16

Example 8: The Blues Progression 18

Example 9: Blues Solo In B♭ 20

Part II: *Fingerings*

Examples 10 & 11 24

Example 12 25

Part III: *String Bending*

Examples 13 & 14 27

Example 15: Blues Scale Bends 28

Example 16: Bending to the 6th 29

Example 17: Bending Between the Minor and Major Third 29

Part IV: *12 Bar Blues Solo*

Example 18: C Minor Pentatonic Fingerings 30

Example 19: C Minor Pentatonic with the Added 6th 31

Example 20: C Minor Pentatonic with the Added ♭5th 32

Example 21: Five Blues Licks 33

Example 22: The Complete Blues Solo in C 35

Part V: *Slo-Mo Blues*

Example 23: 37

Part VI: *Chords and Comping*

Example 24 42

Examples 25 & 26: 44

Example 27 46

Five Chord Voicings for the Blues

Example 28 50

Examples 29 & 30 51

Example 31: Comping Demo over a C Blues 52

Example 32: Comping Demo over a B♭ Blues 55

Example 33: Four More Voicings for the Blues 58

Example 34: 2nd Comping Demo over a B♭ Blues 59

Guitar Tab Glossary 61

INTRODUCTION

Welcome to *Playin' the Blues*. This Book covers all the basics of contemporary blues guitar style. Some of the things we will be looking at in this book are traditional blues progressions, chord voicings, rhythms used in comping, string bending, picking techniques, scales used in blues soloing and many blues licks. For more advanced material refer to my book *The Blues and Beyond* (REHBK001) available from CPP Media.

Part I
Scales For Blues Soloing

Example 1: G Minor Pentatonic

The first scale we are going to examine is the G minor pentatonic scale. All pentatonic scales contain 5 tones as opposed to the diatonic (7 tone) and chromatic (12 tone) scales. The notes in the G minor pentatonic scale are: G, B♭, C, D, & F (1st, ♭3rd, 4th, 5th, & ♭7th degrees of the major scale.)

Here are the two fingerings that Robben demonstrates:

Example 1A:

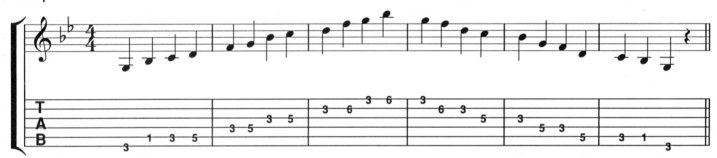

Example 1B:

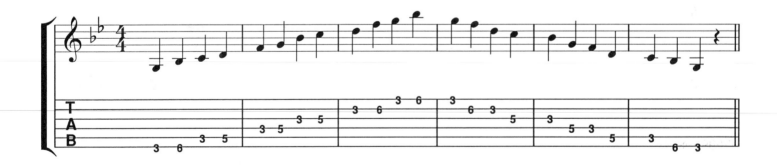

Example 1C: Five Fingerings for G Minor Pentatonic

This example shows the five most common fingerings for the G minor pentatonic scale. Notice that because no open strings are used, each of these fingerings is moveable to any position or key. The root of each scale is indicated with a box. (Example 1B is the same as Fingering #1 and Example 1A is a combination of Fingerings 5 and 1.)

Fingering #1:

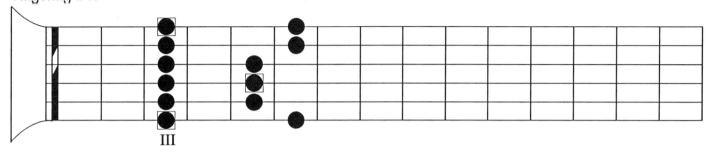

Fingering #2:

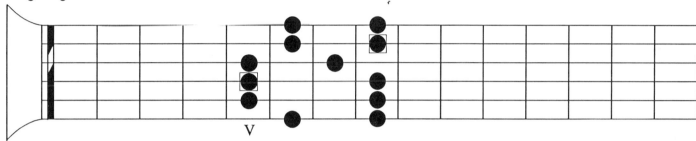

Fingering #3:

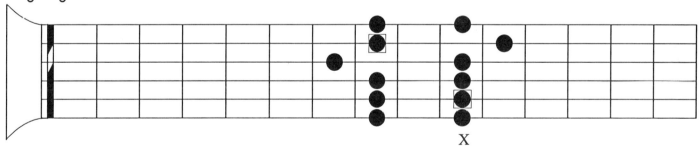

Fingering #4:

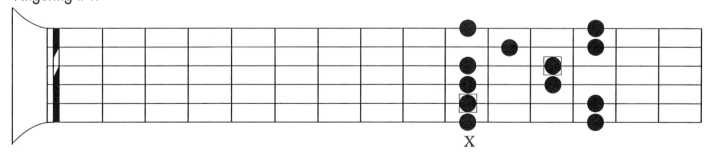

Fingering #5:

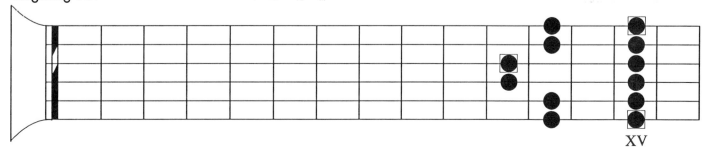

Example 2:
Solo Demonstration over a G7 Vamp

Here, Robben demonstrates the sound of the G minor pentatonic scale by playing it over a bluesy G7 vamp. Often, when playing the B♭ (♭3rd), Robben bends it slightly sharp, getting it right in between the ♭3rd and ♮3rd (bars 3 and 12). This is a very common blues device and adds a hard-edged blues quality to the solo.

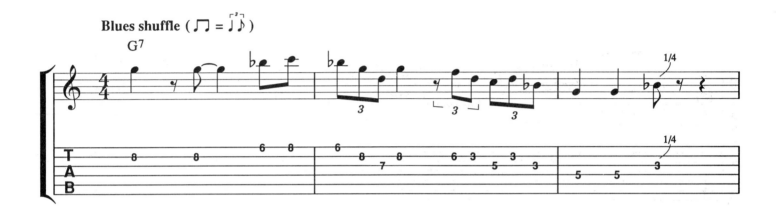

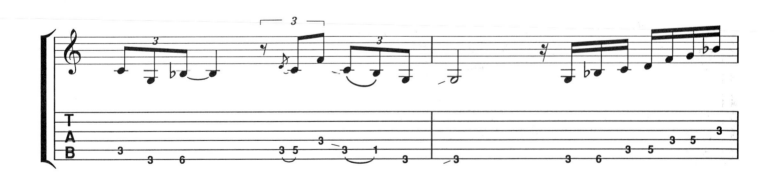

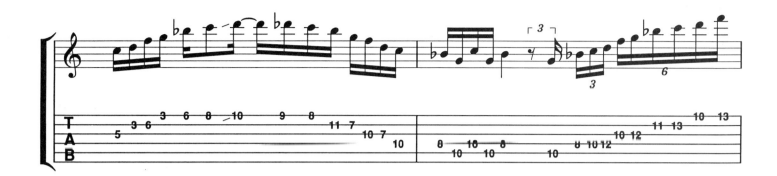

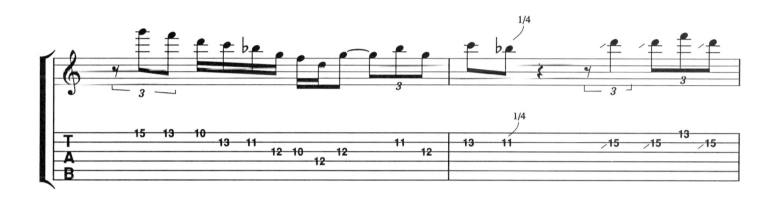

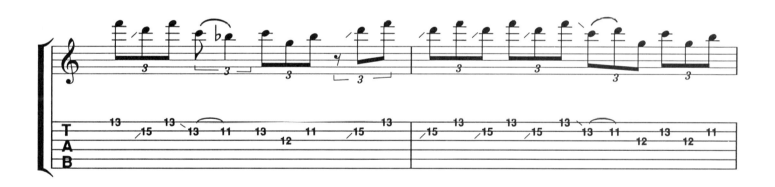

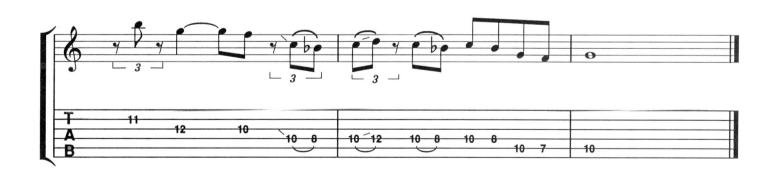

Example 3: G Minor Pentatonic with the ♭5 Added

It is very common to add the ♭5 (♯11) to the minor pentatonic scale. The ♭3rd, ♭7th and ♭5th are known as **"blue notes."** The minor pentatonic scale, with the added ♭5, is often called the **"Blues Scale."** In the G minor pentatonic scale, the added note is D♭.

Here is the "blues scale" fingering as demonstrated by Robben:

Example 3A: Five Fingerings for the G Blues Scale

Fingering #1:

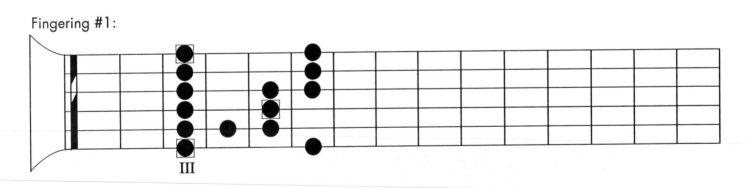

Fingering #2:

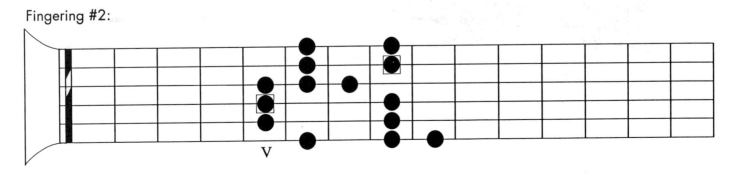

Fingering #3:

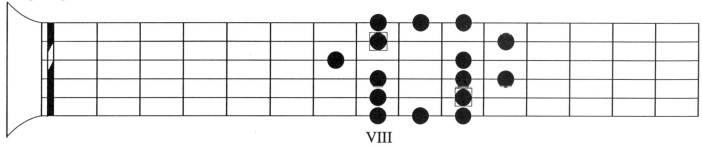

VIII

Fingering #4:

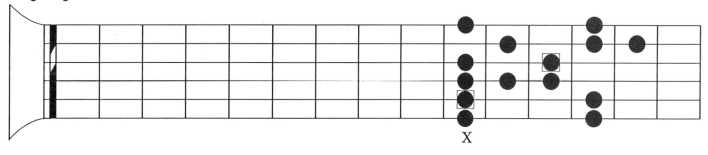

X

Fingering #5:

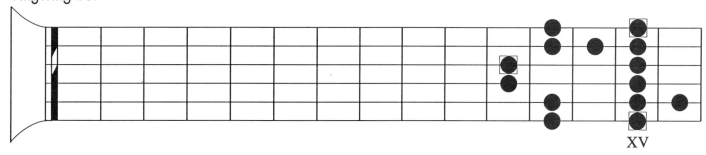

XV

Example 4: Solo Demonstration of the Blues Scale

The following solo demonstrates the use of the blues scale over a G7 vamp. The basic rhythmic feel of this vamp is called a shuffle. In a shuffle, each beat is subdivided into groups of three (triplets).

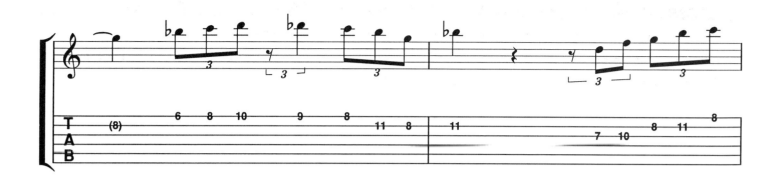

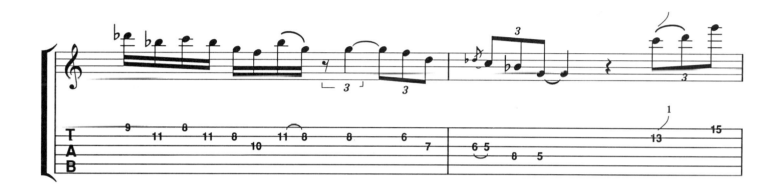

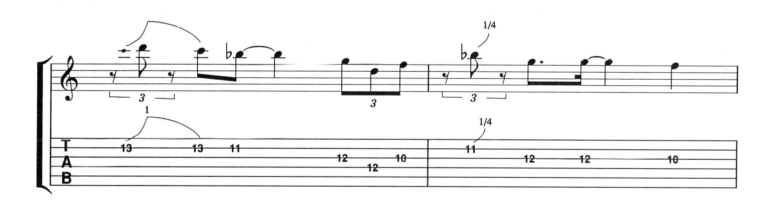

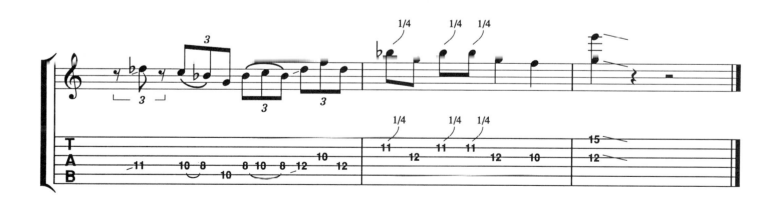

Example 5: G Minor Pentatonic with the Added 6th

The third scale we are going to learn is another variation of the basic pentatonic scale. In this variation the 7th (F) is replaced by the 6th (E).

Here is the fingering Robben demonstrates:

Example 5A:
Five Fingerings for the G Minor Pentatonic with Added 6th

Fingering #1:

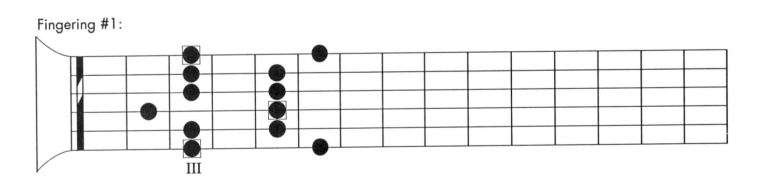

Fingering #2:

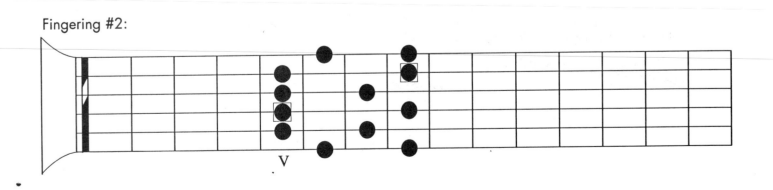

Fingering #3:

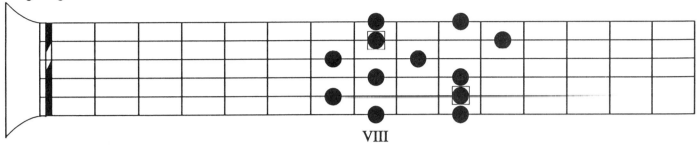

VIII

Fingering #4:

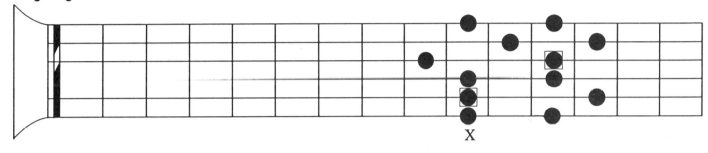

X

Fingering #5:

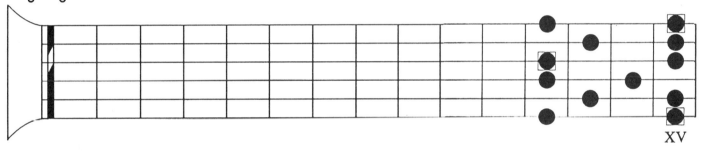

XV

Example 6:
Solo Demonstration of the G Minor Pentatonic with Added 6th

You will notice that this scale has a brighter, more uplifting sound than either the minor pentatonic or blues scales. Both Robben and B.B. King use this scale quite a bit, giving them a "sweet" sound. By contrast, Albert King and Stevie Ray Vaughan both lean heavily on the blues scale with it's characteristic "harsh" quality.

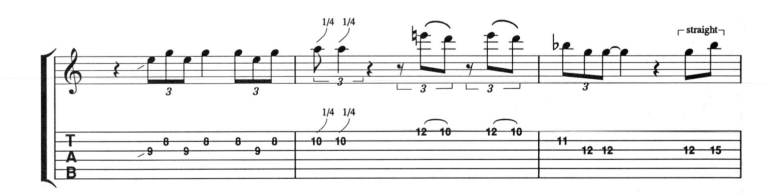

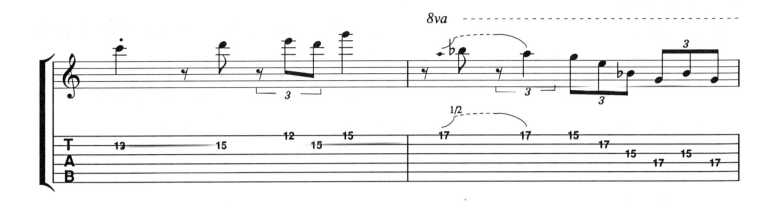

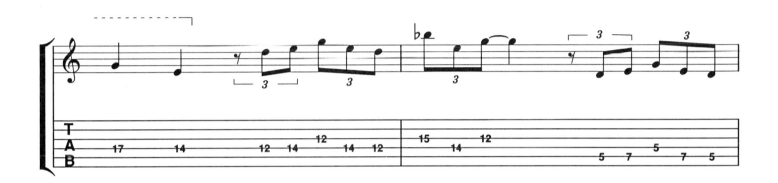

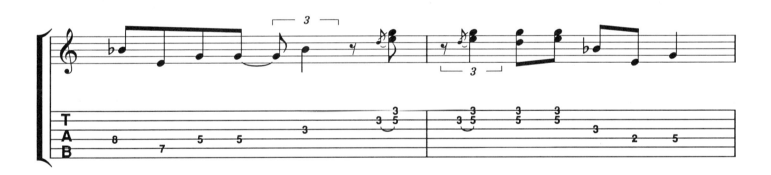

Example 7: Solo Demonstration Using All Three Scales

This example uses all three scales. You will find many examples using the ♭5th and 6th. Especially note how the 6th (E) is used. This note adds a wonderful quality to the solo but is often overlooked by guitarists coming from a rock background.

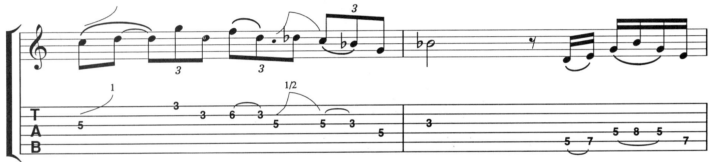

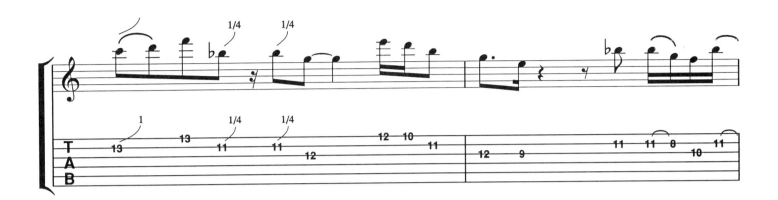

Example 8A: The Blues Progression

This example shows how the notes of the G minor pentatonic scale relate to each of the three chords in a "G Blues." It would be a good idea to record these chords and practice playing the scale over each. Get familiar with how each note of the scale sounds when played against the G7, C7 and D7 chords.

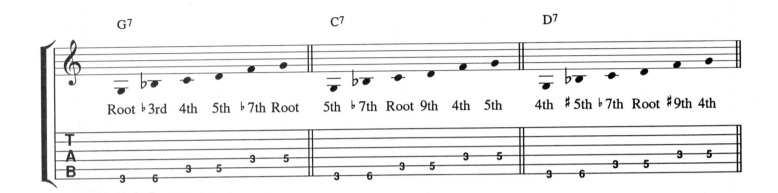

Example 8B

This example shows how the notes in the G blues scale relate to each chord

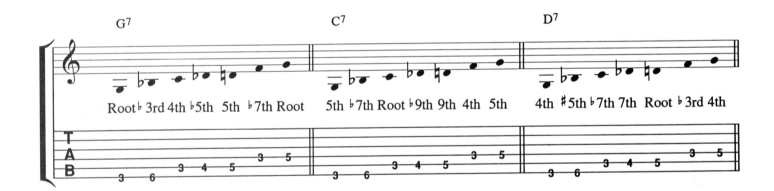

Example 8C

This example shows the relationship of the G minor pentatonic with added 6th to each of the three chords.

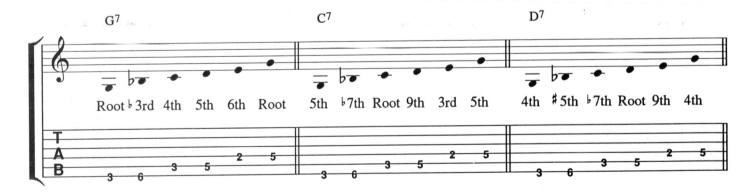

Example 9: Blues Solo in B♭

Here Robben demonstrates how he integrates all three of these scales into his playing. The key has been changed to B♭, so make sure you can transpose all of your fingerings from G to B♭.

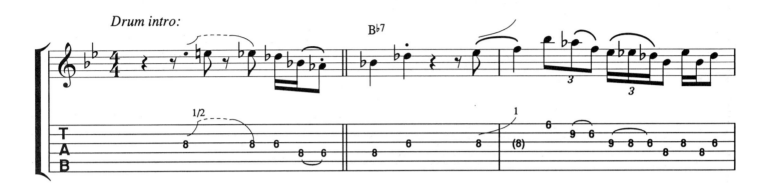

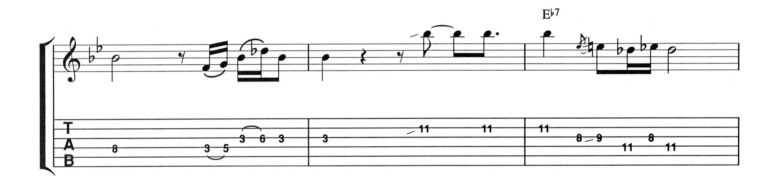

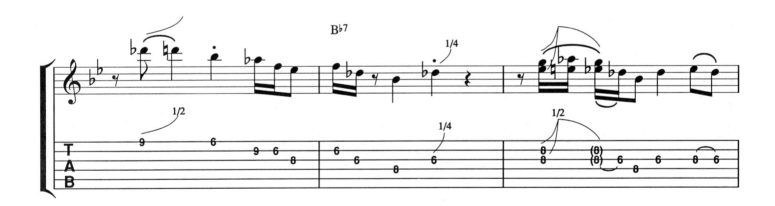

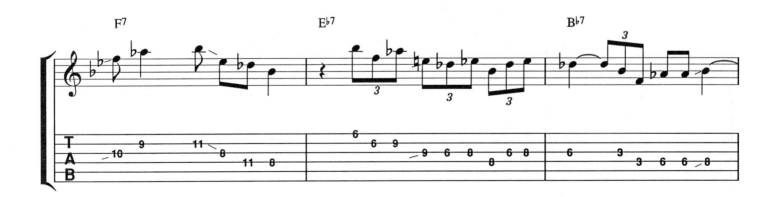

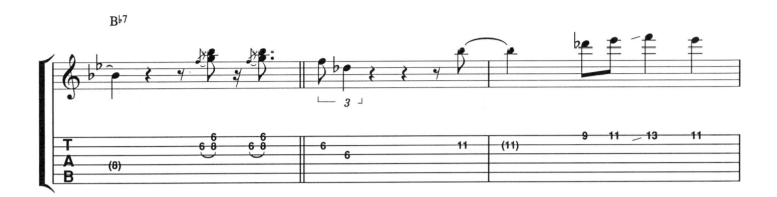

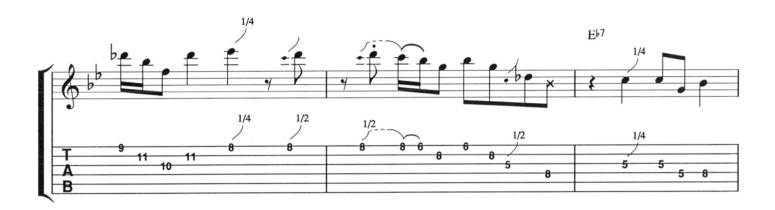

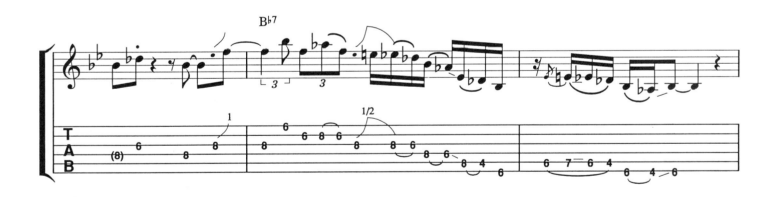

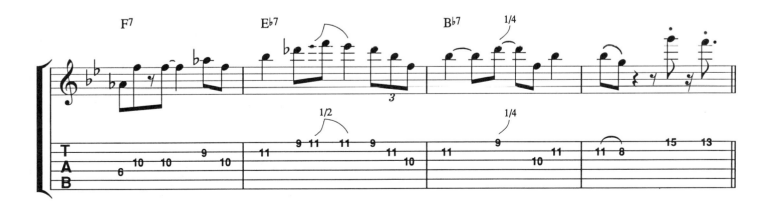

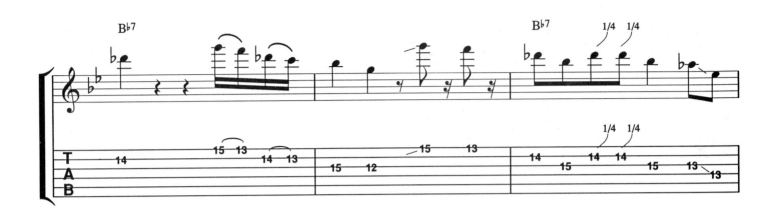

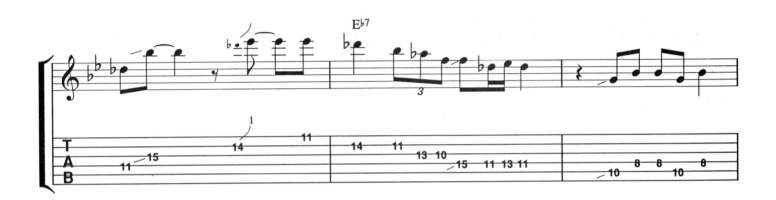

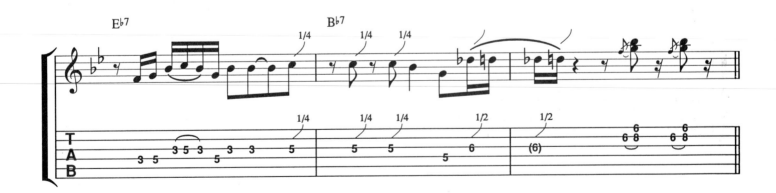

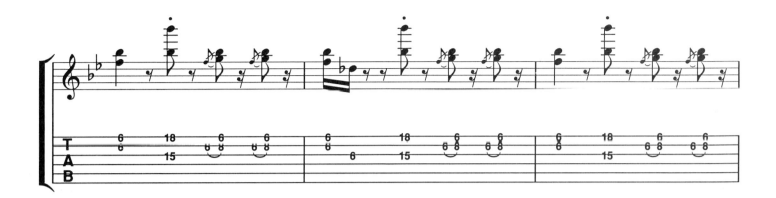

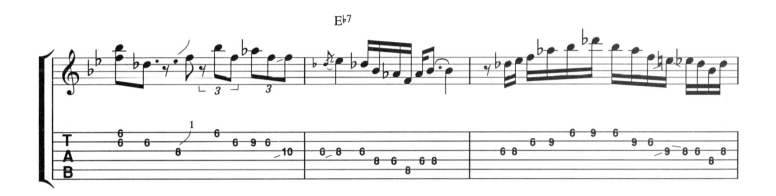

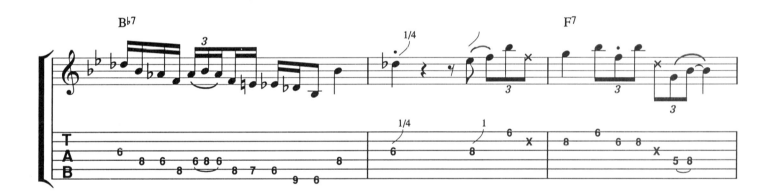

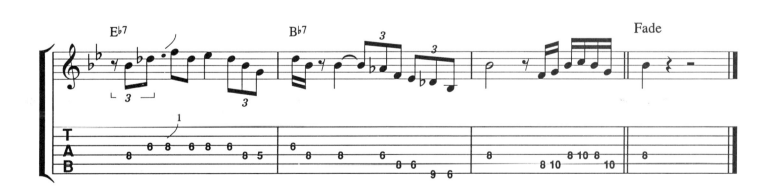

Part II
Fingerings

Very often an artist's own idiosyncratic techniques figure very heavily into their style, feel and sound — helping to set them apart from the crowd. Wes Montgomery, who played with his thumb, and Django Reinhardt, who because of an accident was limited to using only two fingers of his left hand, both developed very individual styles.

Robben often uses just the 1st and 4th fingers of his left hand. The 4th finger is reinforced by the 3rd and sometimes 2nd fingers. This fingering style helps give Robben his characteristic "fat" sound and vibrato.

Example 10

This example shows Robben's left hand fingering for a common blues lick.

Example 11

This "two finger" technique actually developed out of Robben's desire to begin using his 4th finger. Like many guitarists, Robben used to use only his first three fingers. As he began to develop the 4th finger he would support it with his 3rd and sometimes 2nd fingers to give it strength and support. This combination of several fingers on a note adds power to his sound, giving him a very thick, rich tone.

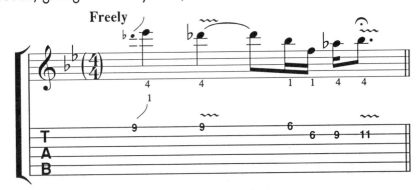

Example 12

Note how Robben "slips and slides" around the neck when using this "two finger" technique. Although this is not the most economical fingering, it adds to the power and feel of his soloing style.

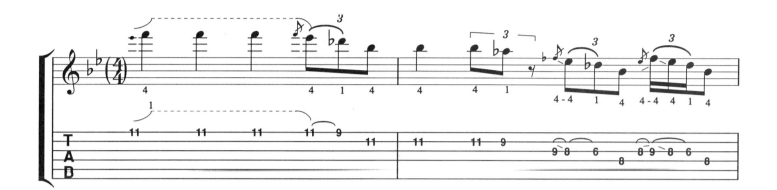

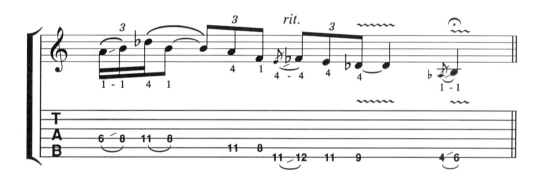

As Robben points out, it is important to develop all of your fingers, especially for other styles of music. But it is interesting to note, that for each different style of music there are many techniques that, while not considered "proper," help to deliver the right feel for that style.

Regarding Robben's vibrato, many blues guitarists prefer to bend a note with the 3rd or 2nd finger and then add vibrato. By contrast, Robben usually adds vibrato on notes that aren't bent. Using the technique of supporting the 4th finger with the 3rd and 2nd, Robben bends the string down slightly (towards the floor) and pivots his entire hand from the wrist to create a rich, vocal-like vibrato.

Part III
String Bending

The art of bending notes is a very important ingredient in the blues style of playing. The notes can be bent many different intervals, from a half step to as much as a perfect fourth. Something that really adds to the character of blues guitar are the "in between" bends, like quarter and three quarter-step bends.

Example 13

This example demonstrates some typical whole step bends.

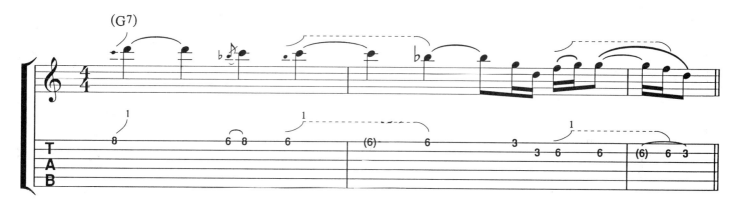

Example 14: Pentatonic Bends

You can bend any note of the pentatonic scale up to the next note in the scale. The following example shows how you can bend each of the notes of the G minor pentatonic scale.

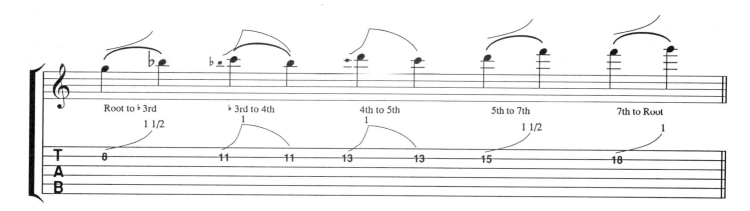

Example 15: Blues Scale Bends

These examples incorporate the flatted fifth. Notice that these are the first examples incorporating a half-step bend.

Example 15A:

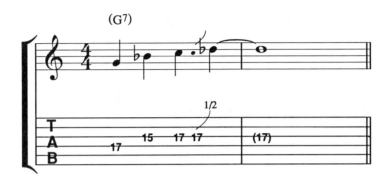

Example 15B:

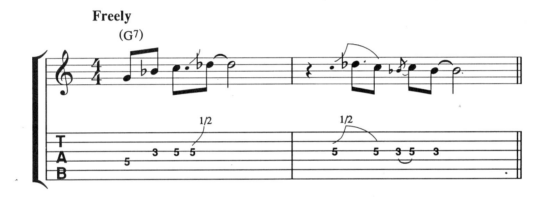

Example 15C:

Example 16: Bending to the 6th

This example highlights the bend from the 5th (D) to the 6th (E). Note that this example also includes the ♭7th and ♭5th.

Example 17: Bending between the Minor and Major Third

A common technique of Robben's, which he attributes to playing with Miles Davis, is the maj3rd/min3rd bend. Listen for how the bend to the major 3rd "brightens" and adds an element of surprise to what could have been a predictable blues scale lick.

Part IV
12 Bar Blues Solo

Here, Robben breaks down a complete blues solo in C, lick-by-lick. Before beginning, let's transpose the fingerings for the three different types of blues scales to C.

Example 18: C Minor Pentatonic Fingerings

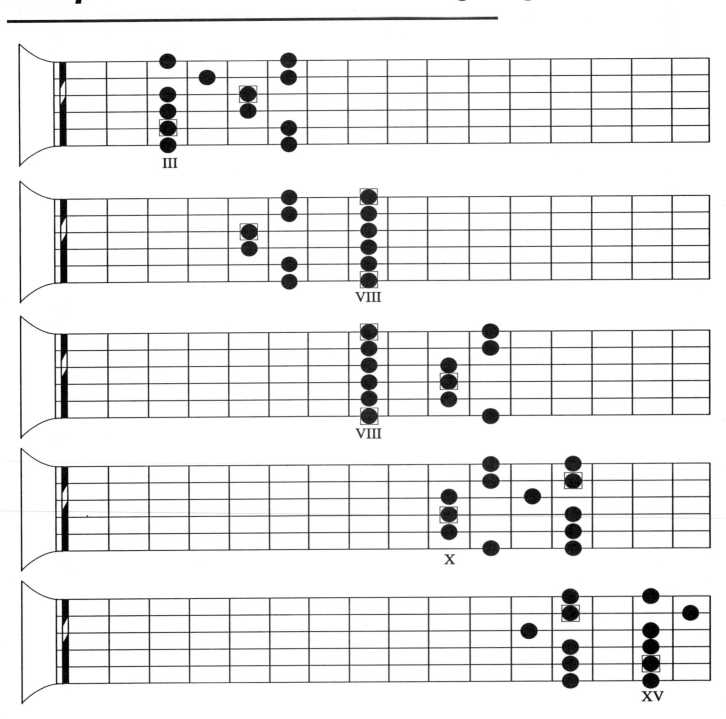

Example 19:
C Minor Pentatonic with the Added 6th

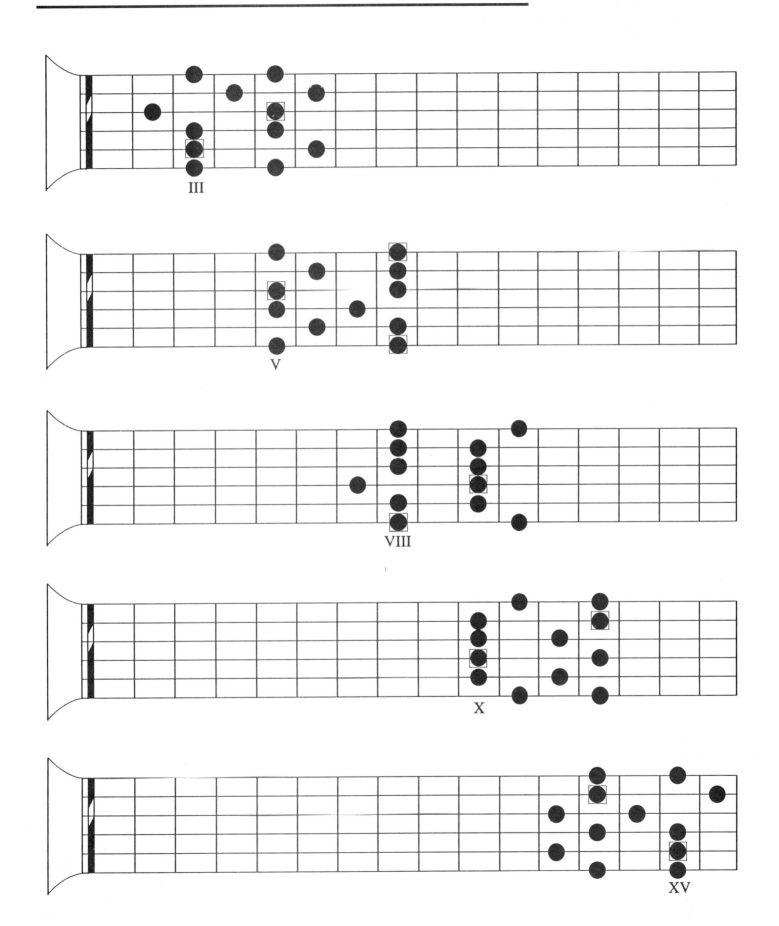

Example 20:
C Minor Pentatonic with the Added ♭5th

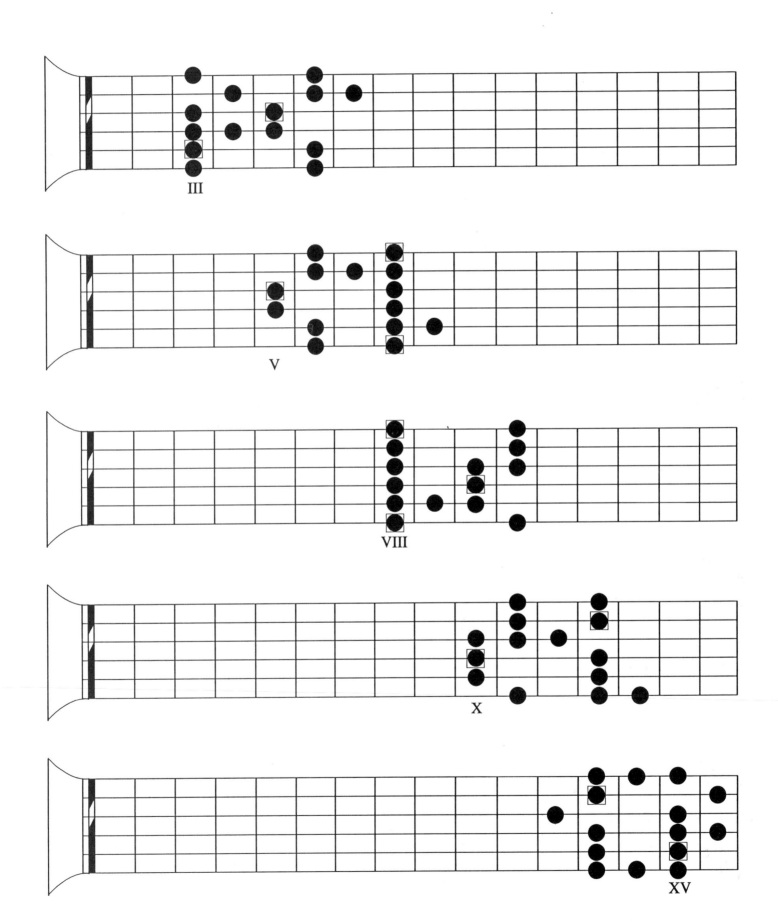

Example 21: Five Blues Licks

The following blues solo is broken down into five licks. Each lick covers an important transition in the blues progression. Lick 1 shows the pickup into the I chord, and Lick 2 the transition from the IV back to the I. Licks 3 and 4 highlight the change from the I to IV and back to I, and Lick 5 covers the change from V to IV.

Licks 1 & 2

Lick 1 is based on the pentatonic scale, including the flatted fifth (G♭). Lick 2 is based on the minor pentatonic with the added sixth (A).

Lick #1

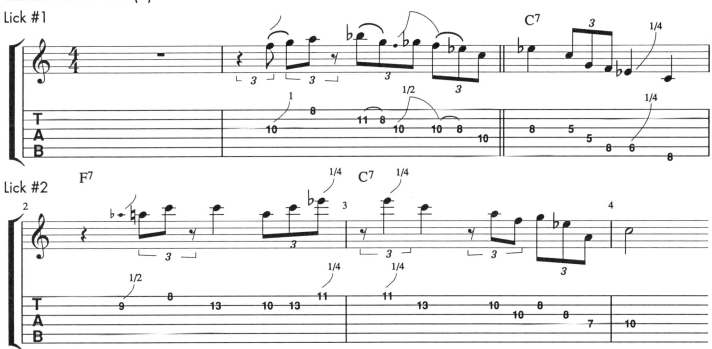

Lick #2

Licks 3 & 4

This next lick works over the transition to the IV chord (F7) and back to the I chord (C7). Notice the use of the 6th (A) over the IV chord. The A is of course the 3rd of the F7 chord.

Lick #3

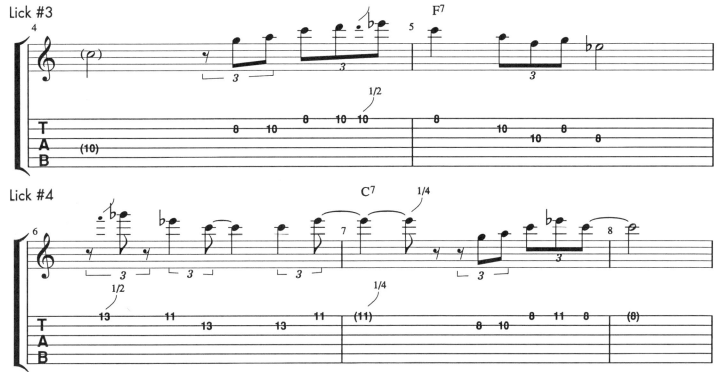

Lick #4

Lick 5

This lick finishes off the 12-bar blues solo. Notice that both the G7 and F7 changes are highlighted by minor 3rd to major 3rd blends.

Lick #5

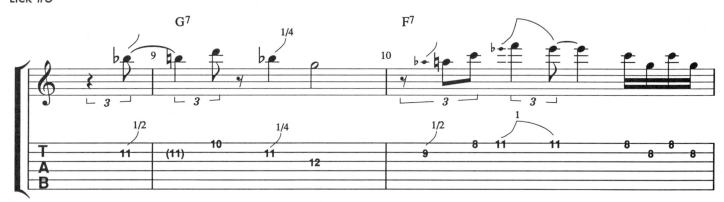

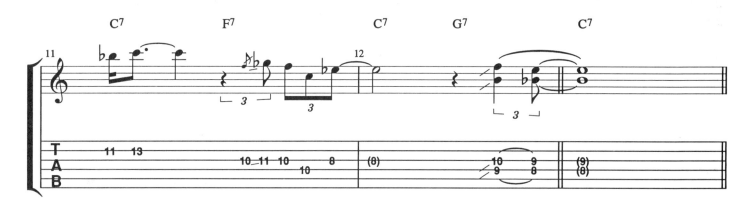

Example 22: The Complete Blues Solo in C

Here we have the complete solo as played on the accompanying recording.

Example 23

Here, Robben plays a slow blues solo, using all of the scales and techniques discussed so far. The slow tempo should make it easier to absorb many of these licks and phrases.

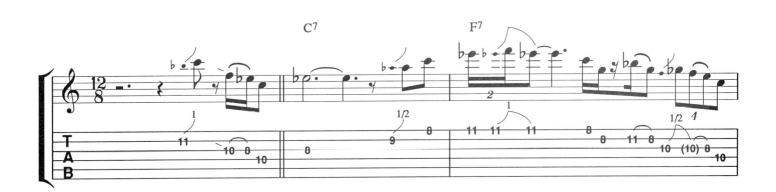

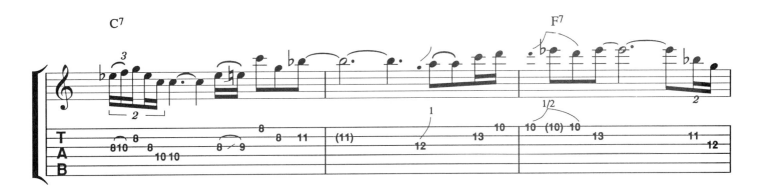

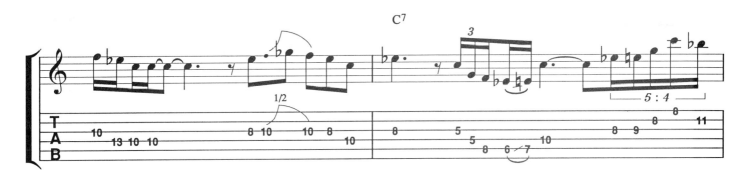

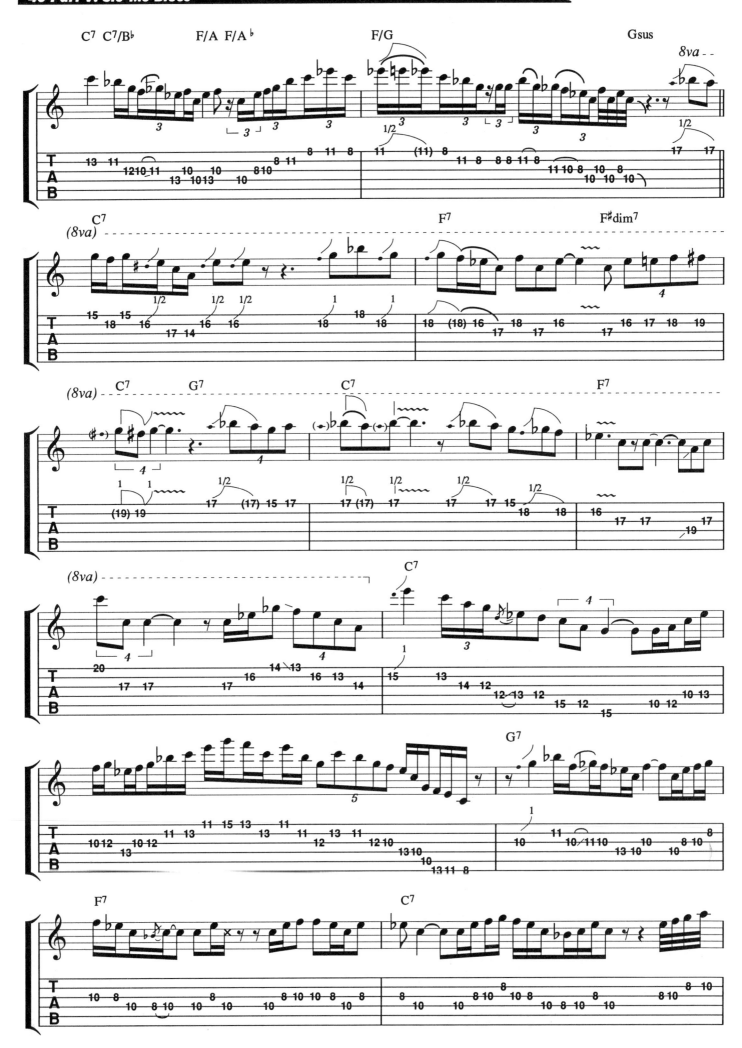

Part VI
Chords and Comping

Example 24

This section examines comping and chord voicings. First let's look at the C mixolydian scale. (The mixolydian scale is the same as a major scale with a ♭7th.) The fretboard diagrams indicate the C mixolydian scale in five fingerings up the neck.

C Mixolydian Scale:

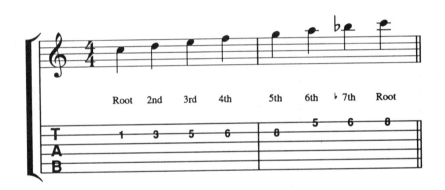

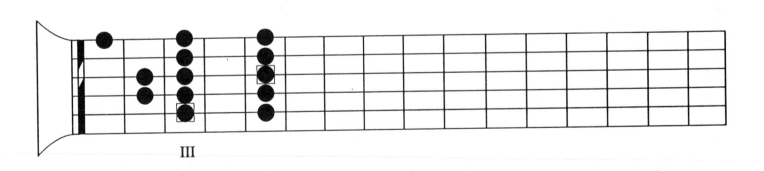

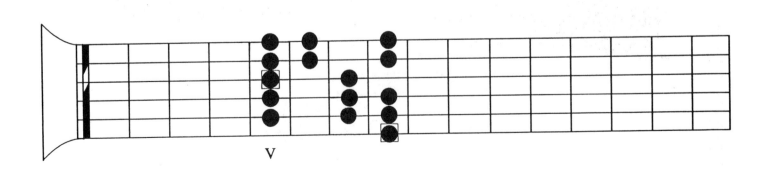

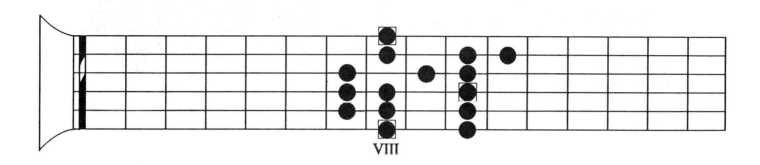

VIII

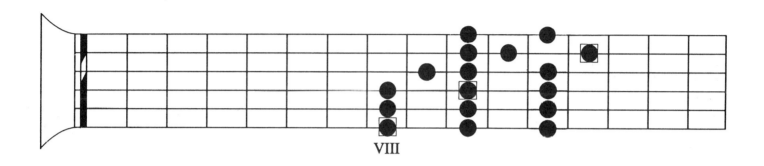

VIII

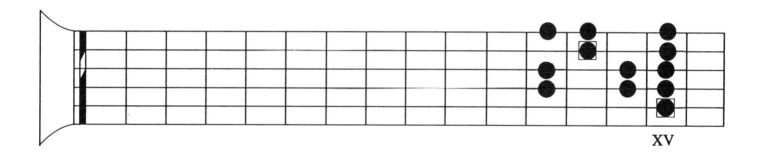

XV

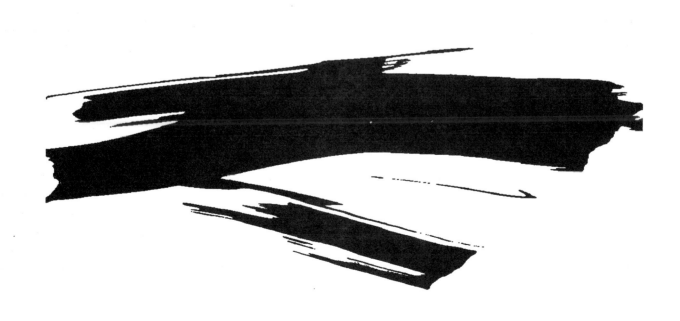

Example 25

Here, the C mixolydian scale is harmonized in sixths:

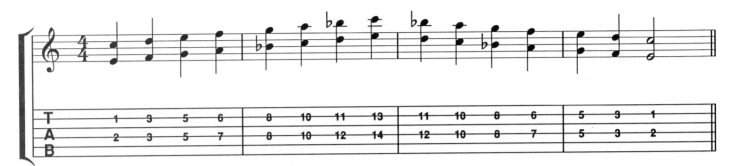

Example 26

Many background figures (and leads) are derived from the interval of a sixth. This example shows how you can use these sixths to form background patterns over a C7 chord vamp.

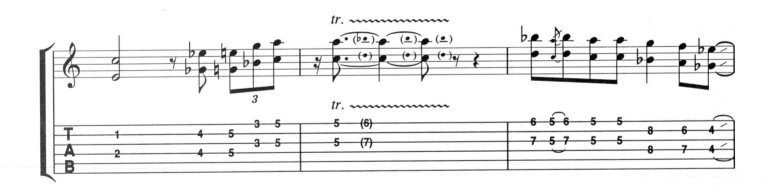

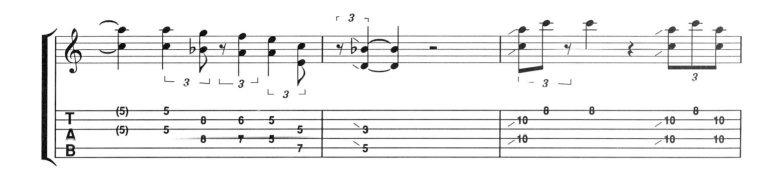

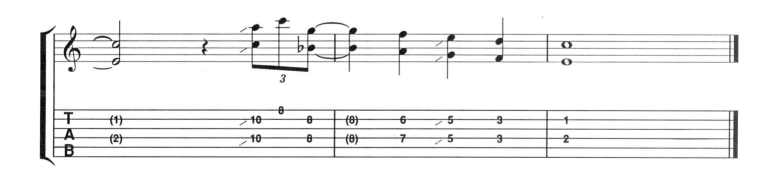

Example 27

In this example, Robben uses sixths to create comping patterns over a 12-bar blues. Each pattern is repetitive in that once a pattern is established for the C7 chord, the same pattern is then transposed to the F7 and G7 chords.

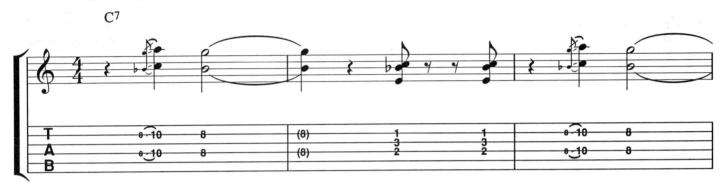

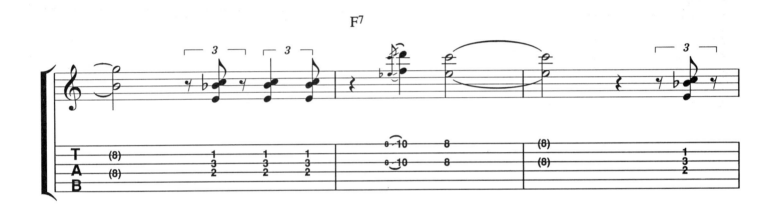

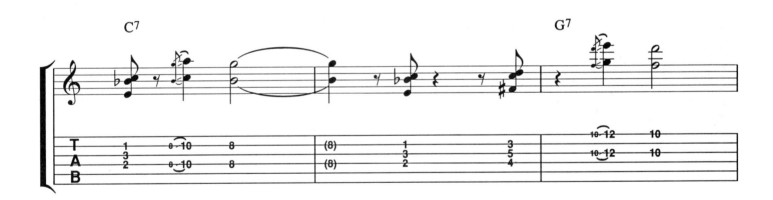

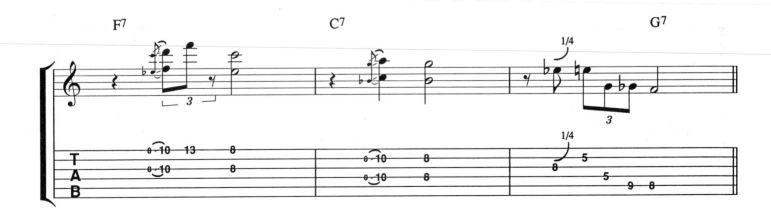

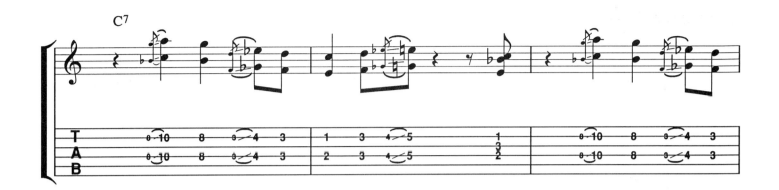

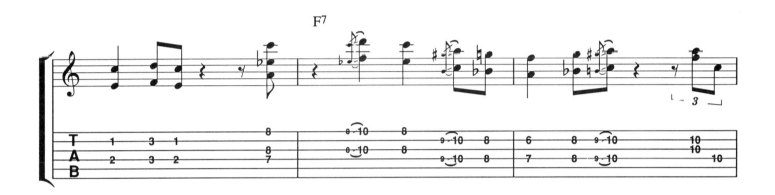

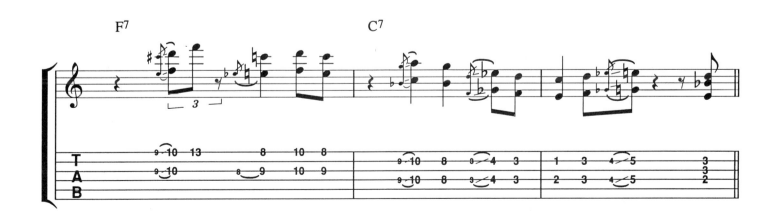

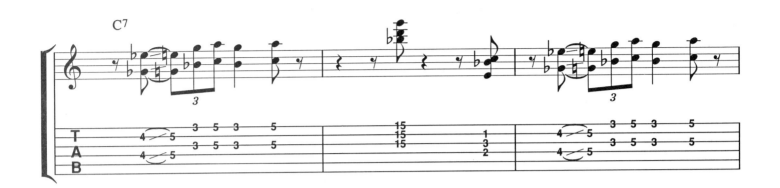

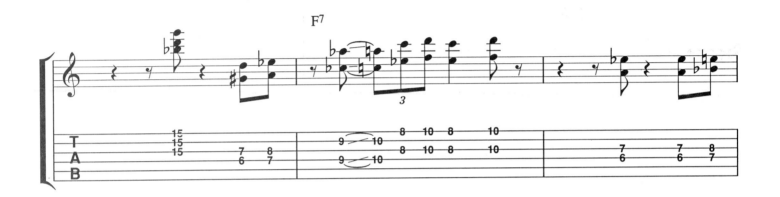

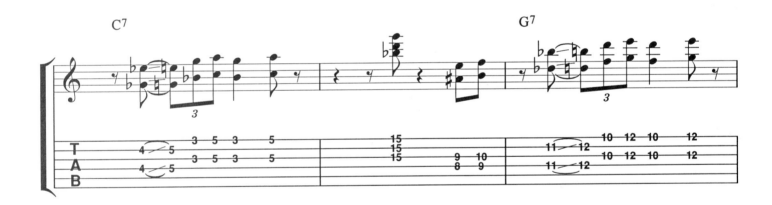

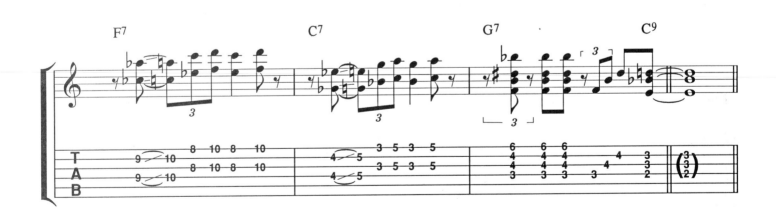

Example 28: Five Chord Voicings for the Blues

These C7 and F chord voicings work especially well together, as shown in the following transcription. This pattern is commonly used over the I7 chord in a blues progression.

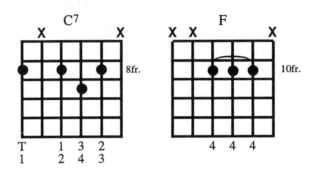

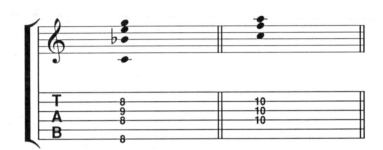

Example 29

This example uses a more sophisticated chord voicing for the C7 change, C13. The 13th is the same scale tone as the 6th (A in the key of C); because it is considered an extension, added on top of the basic chord tones (1, 3, 5, & ♭7), it is considered the 13th rather than the 6th.

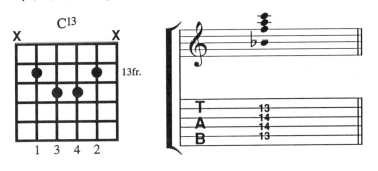

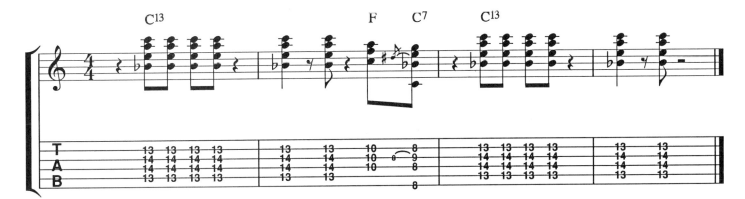

Example 30

This example shows two F9 voicings. The first contains the 3rd, ♭7th, 9th, and 5th. The second voicing is played with a 1st finger barre and contains the ♭7th, 9th, and 5th. Notice that this voicing has no 3rd. The following music example shows a common rhythm pattern using this second voicing.

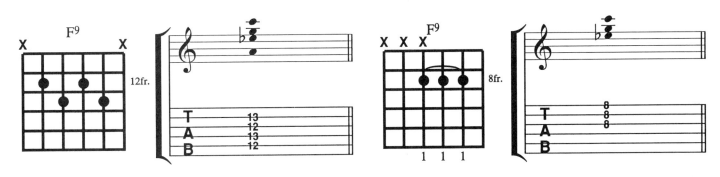

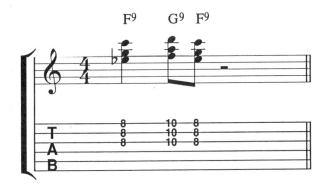

Example 31: Comping Demo over a C Blues

In this example, Robben demonstrates how to utilize the previous five chord voicings to create blues comping patterns. Notice that the patterns are repetitive. This repetition is an important aspect of blues comping. It helps establish a groove that the soloist can then work over.

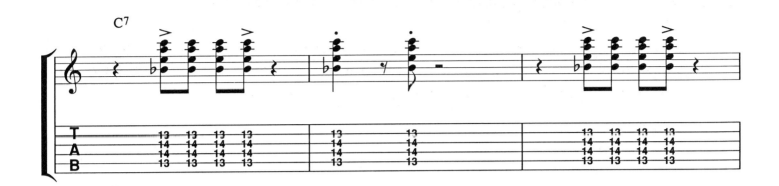

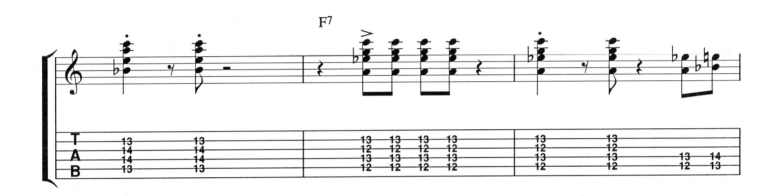

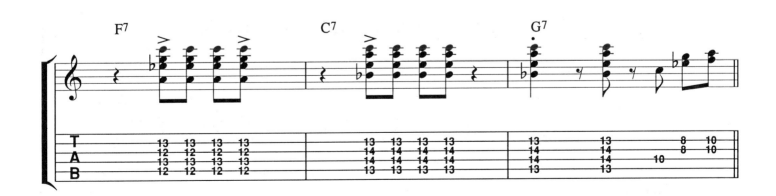

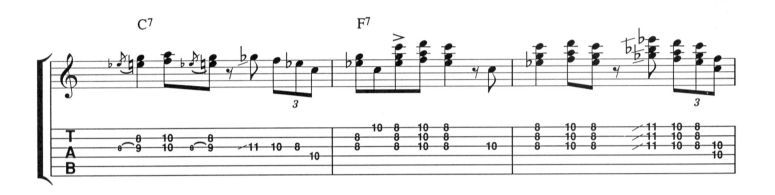

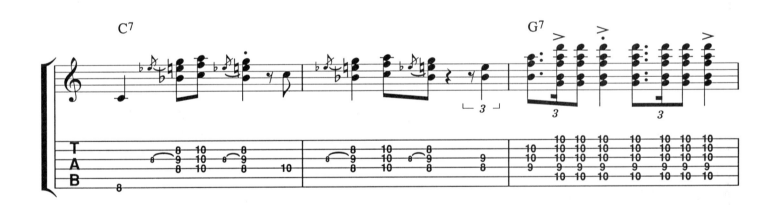

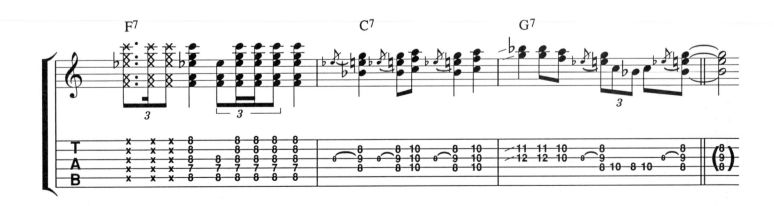

Example 32: Comping Demo over a B♭ Blues

In this example, Robben shows how the same five chord voicings can work in another key, over a different rhythm feel. In the 2nd and 3rd choruses he introduces some of the riffs and patterns first discussed in Examples 23 and 24.

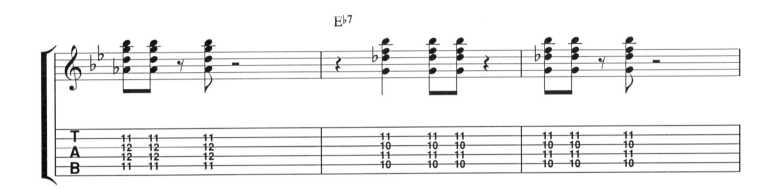

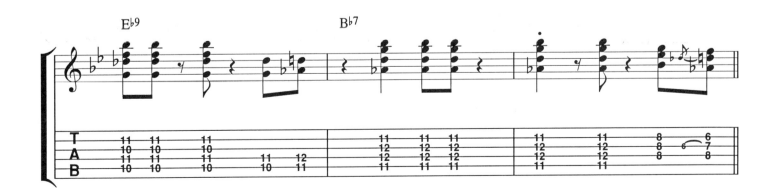

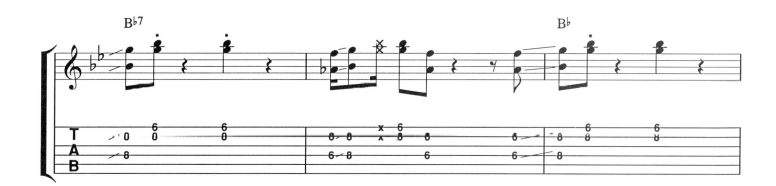

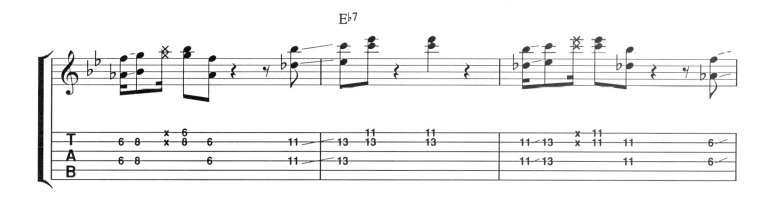

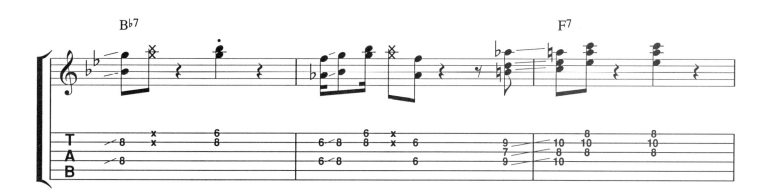

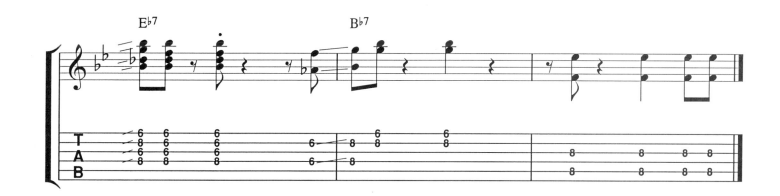

Example 33A - D: Four More Voicings for the Blues

Example 33A:

This is a very useful voicing for the dominant 7th chord. If the chord looks unfamiliar, try sliding it down to 1st position where it would become a C7. Notice that the root is doubled on the top and bottom (2nd and 5th strings) of the chord.

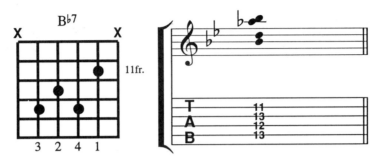

Example 33B:

This is a variation on the previous chord. Here, the 5th string root is replaced by placing F (the 5th of the chord) on the 1st string.

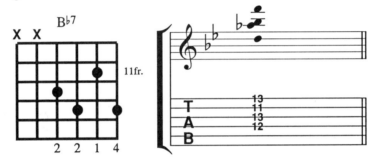

Example 33C:

This form of the 7th chord has the root in the bass and the 3rd on top.

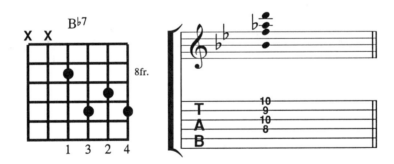

Example 33D:

This voicing for E♭7, with the ♭7th on top, has a very funky blues sound. Of course, by sliding it up two frets you get the F7 (V7) chord.

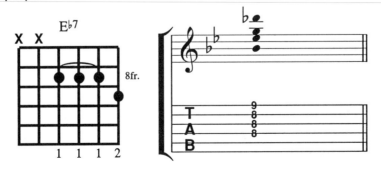

Example 34: 2nd Comping Demo over a B♭ Blues

In this example, Robben uses the four new voicings, plus a few of the previous, to comp over an up tempo, funky blues feel.

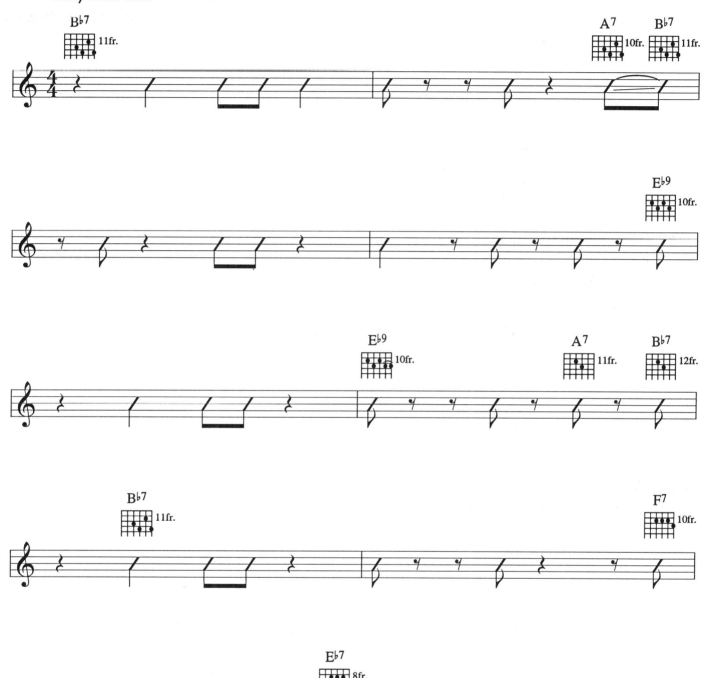

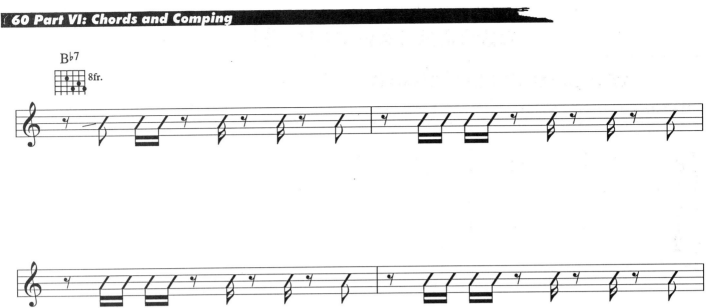

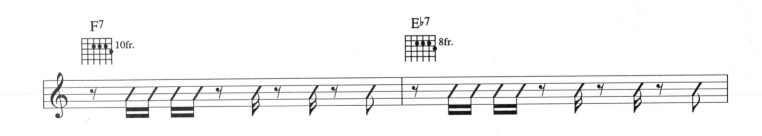

GUITAR TAB GLOSSARY **

TABLATURE EXPLANATION

READING TABLATURE: Tablature illustrates the six strings of the guitar. Notes and chords are indicated by the placement of fret numbers on a given string(s).

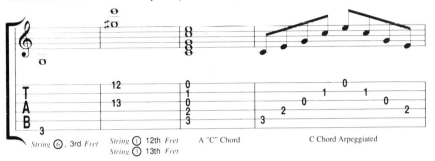

String ⑥, 3rd *Fret*   String ① 12th *Fret*   A "C" Chord   C Chord Arpeggiated
String ③ 13th *Fret*

BENDING NOTES

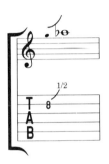

HALF STEP: Play the note and bend string one half step.*

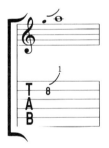

WHOLE STEP: Play the note and bend string one whole step.

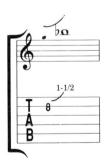

WHOLE STEP AND A HALF: Play the note and bend string a whole step and a half.

TWO STEPS: Play the note and bend string two whole steps.

SLIGHT BEND (Microtone): Play the note and bend string slightly to the equivalent of half a fret.

PREBEND (Ghost Bend): Bend to the specified note, before the string is picked.

PREBEND AND RELEASE: Bend the string, play it, then release to the original note.

REVERSE BEND: Play the already-bent string, then immediately drop it down to the fretted note.

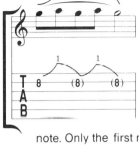

BEND AND RELEASE: Play the note and gradually bend to the next pitch, then release to the original note. Only the first note is attacked.

BENDS INVOLVING MORE THAN ONE STRING: Play the note and bend string while playing an additional note (or notes) on another string(s). Upon release, relieve pressure from additional note(s), causing original note to sound alone.

BENDS INVOLVING STATIONARY NOTES: Play notes and bend lower pitch, then hold until release begins (indicated at the point where line becomes solid).

UNISON BEND: Play both notes and immediately bend the lower note to the same pitch as the higher note.

DOUBLE NOTE BEND: Play both notes and immediately bend both strings simultaneously.

*A half step is the smallest interval in Western music; it is equal to one fret. A whole step equals two frets.

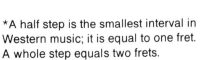

© 1990 Beam Me Up Music
c/o CPP/Belwin, Inc. Miami, Florida 33014
International Copyright Secured   Made in U.S.A.   All Rights Reserved   **By Kenn Chipkin and Aaron Stang

RHYTHM SLASHES

STRUM INDICA-TIONS: Strum with indicated rhythm.
The chord voicings are found on the first page of the transcription underneath the song title.

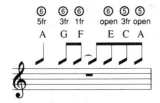

INDICATING SINGLE NOTES USING RHYTHM SLASHES: Very often single notes are incorporated into a rhythm part. The note name is indicated above the rhythm slash with a fret number and a string indication.

ARTICULATIONS

HAMMER ON: Play lower note, then "hammer on" to higher note with another finger. Only the first note is attacked.

LEFT HAND HAMMER: Hammer on the first note played on each string with the left hand.

PULL OFF: Play higher note, then "pull off" to lower note with another finger. Only the first note is attacked.

FRET-BOARD TAPPING: "Tap" onto the note indicated by + with a finger of the pick hand, then pull off to the following note held by the fret hand.

TAP SLIDE: Same as fretboard tapping, but the tapped note is slid randomly up the fretboard, then pulled off to the following note.

BEND AND TAP TECHNIQUE: Play note and bend to specified interval. While holding bend, tap onto note indicated.

LEGATO SLIDE: Play note and slide to the following note. (Only first note is attacked).

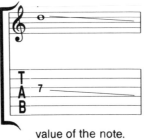

LONG GLISSAN-DO: Play note and slide in specified direction for the full value of the note.

SHORT GLISSAN-DO: Play note for its full value and slide in specified direction at the last possible moment.

PICK SLIDE: Slide the edge of the pick in specified direction across the length of the string(s).

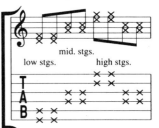

MUTED STRINGS: A percussive sound is made by laying the fret hand across all six strings while pick hand strikes specified area (low, mid, high strings).

PALM MUTE: The note or notes are muted by the palm of the pick hand by lightly touching the string(s) near the bridge.

TREMOLO PICKING: The note or notes are picked as fast as possible.

TRILL: Hammer on and pull off consecutively and as fast as possible between the original note and the grace note.

ACCENT: Notes or chords are to be played with added emphasis.

STACCATO (Detached Notes): Notes or chords are to be played roughly half their actual value and with separation.

DOWN STROKES AND UPSTROKES: Notes or chords are to be played with either a downstroke (⊓ ·) or upstroke (∨) of the pick.

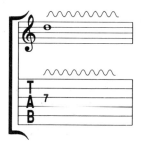

VIBRATO: The pitch of a note is varied by a rapid shaking of the fret hand finger, wrist, and forearm.

HARMONICS

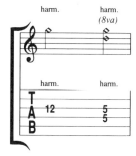

NATURAL HARMONIC: A finger of the fret hand lightly touches the note or notes indicated in the tab and is played by the pick hand.

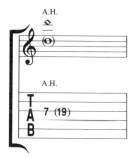

ARTIFICIAL HARMONIC: The first tab number is fretted, then the pick hand produces the harmonic by using a finger to lightly touch the same string at the second tab number (in parenthesis) and is then picked by another finger.

ARTIFICIAL "PINCH" HAR-MONIC: A note is fretted as indicated by the tab, then the pick hand produces the harmonic by squeezing the pick firmly while using the tip of the index finger in the pick attack. If parenthesis are found around the fretted note, it does not sound. No parenthesis means both the fretted note and A.H. are heard simultaneously.

TREMOLO BAR

SPECIFIED INTERVAL: The pitch of a note or chord is lowered to a specified interval and then may or may not return to the original pitch. The activity of the tremolo bar is graphically represented by peaks and valleys.

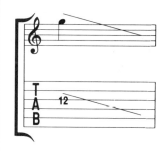

UN-SPECIFIED INTERVAL: The pitch of a note or a chord is lowered to an unspecified interval.

Available from CPP Media Group

Books with Audio

Robben Ford   The Blues and Beyond
(REHBK001AT) with Cassette
(REHBK001CD) with CD

Playin' the Blues   (REHBK004AT) with Cassette
(REHBK004CD) with CD

Yngwie Malmsteen   (REHBK002AT) with Cassette
(REHBK002CD) with CD

Paul Gilbert   Intense Rock II
(REHBK003AT) with Cassette
(REHBK003CD) with CD

Videos

Robben Ford   The Blues and Beyond (REH821)
Playin' the Blues (REH801)

Yngwie Malmsteen   (REH819)

Paul Gilbert   Intense Rock Sequences & Techniques (REH805)
Intense Rock II (REH822)

For a complete catalog, contact:
CPP MEDIA GROUP
15800 N.W. 48th Avenue
Miami, Florida 33014